Culture

LIVING IN THE PLACES OF GOD

Scott Nelson

Foreword by Alan Hirsch

FORGE GUIDES FOR MISSIONAL CONVERSATION

IVP Connect

An imprint of InterVarsity Press
Downers Grove, Illinois

InterVarsity Press
P.O. Box 1400, Downers Grove, IL 60515-1426
World Wide Web: www.ivpress.com
E-mail: email@ivpress.com

InterVarsity Press® is the book-publishing division of InterVarsity Christian Fellowship/USA®, a movement of students and faculty active on campus at hundreds of universities, colleges and schools of nursing in the United States of America, and a member movement of the International Fellowship of Evangelical Students. For information about local and regional activities, write Public Relations Dept., InterVarsity Christian Fellowship/USA, 6400 Schroeder Rd., P.O. Box 7895, Madison, WI 53707-7895, or visit the IVCF website at <www.intervarsity.org>.

All Scripture quotations, unless otherwise indicated, are taken from the Holy Bible, New International Version®, NIV® Copyright © 1973, 1978, 1984, 2011 by Biblica, Inc.™ Used by permission. All rights reserved worldwide.

While all stories in this book are true, some names and identifying information in this book have been changed to protect the privacy of the individuals involved.

Cover design: Cindy Kiple

Interior design: Beth Hagenberg

Images: © PhotoHamster/iStockphoto

ISBN 978-0-8308-1045-1 (print)
ISBN 978-0-8308-9571-7 (digital)

Printed in the United States of America ∞

Library of Congress Cataloging-in Publication Data

Nelson, Scott, 1983-
   Culture: living in the places of God / Scott Nelson; foreword by Alan
Hirsch.
      pages cm.—(Forge guides for missional conversation)
   Includes bibliographical references.
   ISBN 978-0-8308-1045-1 (pbk.: alk. paper)
   1. Christianity and culture—Textbooks. 2. Evangelistic
work—Textbooks. I. Title.
BR115.C8N445 2013
261—dc23

                                                          2013018276

| P | 20 | 19 | 18 | 17 | 16 | 15 | 14 | 13 | 12 | 11 | 10 | 9 | 8 | 7 | 6 | 5 | 4 | 3 | 2 | 1 |
| Y | 30 | 29 | 28 | 27 | 26 | 25 | 24 | 23 | 22 | 21 | 20 | 19 | 18 | 17 | 16 | 15 | 14 | 13 |

CONTENTS

FOREWORD

For the better part of two decades now, *missional* has been equal parts buzzword and byword in the contemporary church. Many church leaders have decried the trendiness of the term, predicting that it will eventually go the way of all fads, and that responsible church leadership involves simply waiting it out, keeping the faith. And it's hard to deny the trendiness of the term: as the editors of *Leadership Journal* noted in their preface to an article of mine five years ago, "A quick search on Google uncovers the presence of 'missional communities,' 'missional leaders,' 'missional worship,' even 'missional seating,' and 'missional coffee.'"[1] The closer the application of the term approaches absurdity, the less seriously we are inclined to take it.

And yet over the same period the concept of a missional church has proved its durability. Conference after conference has organized itself around the concept that God is on mission in the world, and that as means to the end of achieving his mission God has created a church. Seminary after seminary has reconfigured its core curricula to take the model of a church on mission seriously, and to train pastors and other leaders to understand themselves as missionaries first, "keepers" of the faith a distant second. What so many have dismissed as a fad or a trend, substantial and growing numbers of people are recognizing as a paradigm shift.

Of course, any number of paradigm-shifting conversations are taking place at the conceptual level among the leadership of the global church at any given moment. Many such conversations bubble up only to dissipate; such in-house deliberation is part of the long history of the faith. It is in this historical reality that the durability and trajectory of the missional church conversation reveals its significance. More than a mere theoretical conversation, the missional church bears the marks of a true movement—broad-based, but with a cohesive sense of self-understanding; goal-driven, but deeply rooted in principles and conviction; critical of the status quo, yet always motivated by the greater good. Christianity itself has always been a movement, inspired by the God who created the world and called it good, who so loved the world that he gave his only Son for it.

Any movement over time has the capacity to atrophy, to be distracted by its own sense of self-preservation, to be enthralled by the beauty of its past accomplishments and the currency of its cultural power. But the original vision of the movement relentlessly beckons, confronting our self-congratulation and propelling us toward the greater good of our original calling.

At Forge we have always said that the best critique of the bad is the practice of the better. With this series of guides on missional practices we are trying to help create a more productive and better future for a church now in systemic decline. We believe the church was made for far more than mere self-preservation, and certainly not for retreat. We were made to be a highly transformative Jesus movement; we had best get on with being that. To do this we need to redisciple the church into its calling and mission. Discipleship is a huge key, and for this we need tools.

Every movement requires the education—the *formation*—of its people. I believe the next phase of the movement that is the missional church resides not so much in seminaries or elder meetings as around the tables of people of faith wherever they find themselves. These Forge Guides for Missional Conversation are intended to facilitate those conversations—to help you, wherever you are, to step together into the flow of God's mission in the world.

Scott Nelson is particularly equipped to facilitate such conversations. He has held leadership positions in traditional churches and studied the church's mission while pursuing his doctorate. He has taken on the responsibility of the theological direction of Forge Mission Training Network in America even as he has developed a missional community in the neighborhood where he lives. The mission of God is thoroughly integrated into Scott's life—heart and soul, mind and strength—which is as it is intended to be.

Each of the five guides that make up this series will be valuable on its own; thoroughly scriptural, accessibly theological, highly practical and fundamentally spiritual, each will give you a fuller appreciation of what it means to be a follower of Jesus on God's mission. Taken together, however, they are a sort of curriculum for a movement: you and your friends will be fully equipped for every good work that God has in mind for you in the place where you find yourself.

Our missionary God created a church in service to his mission. We were made for a movement. Read on if you're ready to move!

Alan Hirsch

INTRODUCTION
TO THE FORGE GUIDES

I've been obsessed with the idea of helping Christians develop a missionary imagination for their daily lives ever since I began to develop such an imagination back in 2007. My missionary imagination began at a church staff retreat. I was asked what I thought our church staff should do if God dropped us all from a helicopter into our city with absolutely no resources and asked us to start a church. While thinking of my answer to this question, I realized I would have to take on the mindset of a missionary—go out to the people, learn who they are, get involved in their lives, care about what they care about. The years that have passed since that fateful question have been an amazing journey for me. I quit my job, dove into full-time study of the missionary mindset in Christian congregations, began exploring ways to live like a missionary in the condominium complex where my wife and I currently live, and teamed up with the Forge America Mission Training Network to be a part of an organization that actively seeks to implant a missionary mindset in Christians and their faith communities.

I've written these guides to help you ask some of the same questions that I asked, and to help you think about what it might look like if you, your group or your church were to develop a missionary imagination for everyday living. There are at least three reasons why it is crucially important that you ask these questions and develop a missionary imagination.

The first reason is the cultural changes that are taking place in Western contexts. Changes such as increasing globalization, religious and cultural pluralism, huge advances in science and technology, the collapse of many modern principles and the growth of postmodernism, and the secularization of the West have drastically altered many cultural landscapes. If the gospel is to be proclaimed faithfully and effectively in these changing contexts, Christians must be missionaries who study cultures in order to translate the gospel so that all can clearly hear it. Simply saying and doing the same things in the same ways as generations past is no longer effective.

A second reason it is vitally important for Christians to develop a missionary mindset is the crisis facing the institutional church. The many different statistical studies that measure the size and influence of the church in the United States are sobering. Despite the explosion of megachurches, congregations in the United States as a whole consist of older people and fewer participants, and experience decreased influence in local contexts. The institutional, established church is experiencing a serious internal crisis as contexts change and congregations fail to adapt. Christians must regain a sense of their missionary calling if the trend of a diminishing role for the Christian faith is to be reversed in the West.

Third, I see evidence of a common longing for a deeper, lived-out faith among many Christians, especially among emerging generations. I've felt it and so have many others who I have read and talked with. It is the feeling that something about the way I am participating in church and faith seems to be missing; it seems to be too easy or too shallow. Conversations with Christians across the country reveal a longing to be challenged, to do something significant with their faith, to make a difference in the lives of people both globally and locally. By developing a missionary imagination for everyday living, these Christians develop a mindset that can lead to deeper expressions of faith, which ultimately reorient a person's whole life around what God is doing and wants to do in this world.

My life story and the three reasons I just listed compelled me to write and use these conversation guides for my own small group. Perhaps you have had a similar experience, or maybe one of the three reasons prompted you to pick up the guides. Even if not, I sincerely hope the questions contained in these guides will infect your minds, as they did mine. And I sincerely hope the mission of God will infect your lives, as I pray every day for it to infect mine.

USING THE FORGE GUIDES

My focus in creating these guides has not been to give you all the answers. I firmly believe you and the members of your group need to discern the answers for yourselves, and further, to generate the creativity that will shape your imagination for what a missionary lifestyle might look like in your life and community. My task in creating these guides is to help you ask good questions.

While creating these guides, I kept coming back to the idea of minimalist running shoes. The science behind these increasingly popular shoes claims that the human body is naturally equipped to run. Big, cushiony, fancy running shoes are not only unnecessary but counterproductive. What runners really need is a simple shoe that accentuates their natural abilities, encourages proper running form and protects their feet from environmental hazards.

These guides are designed to be a lot like minimalist running shoes. They offer the bare minimum you will need to ask good questions, seek innovative answers and develop a new imagination. The guides do not do the work for you. Rather, let them draw out your natural ability to hear from Scripture, to think about the world around you, to wonder about who God is and to imagine ways you can live as a missionary.

These four practices appear in each lesson under the headings

"Dwelling in the Word," "Contextual Analysis," "Theological Reflection" and "Missionary Imagination." I have identified relevant biblical texts, but it is your job to listen for how God is speaking to you and your group. The guides also provide probing questions about your local context, but it is your job to do the analysis required to provide the answers. Similarly, the guides will provide theological content and point to basic principles of missional living, but it is your job to reflect on the nature of God and how he is asking you to live out his mission in your context.

To help you understand what you will be doing as you work through the conversation guides, a brief description of each basic practice follows. Please note that some groups will naturally gravitate to some of the practices more than to others. Don't feel the need to go through each section with a fine-toothed comb. There is more material than will likely be needed for most group gatherings, so be flexible with the practices and allow the group to choose how much time to allocate to each section.

Practice 1: Dwelling in the Word

Each group gathering begins with a time to hear from Scripture through communal reading and listening.[2] Dwelling in the same text over a period of six weeks (or more!) will allow your group to begin developing a shared imagination and a shared openness to the many things God may want to say and do through the text.

The group listens to the passage, reflects in silence for a few moments and then breaks into pairs to discuss two questions about the text. After sufficient time has passed (while allowing adequate time for the remainder of the session), the group gathers together. Individuals share what their partners heard in the text while answers are recorded. This section concludes with the group asking, What might God be up to in this passage for us today?

Sometimes people will doubt the value of returning to the same text time after time, but trust the process and believe that the Bible is the living Word of God. The more you continue to return to the same text, the more you will find blessing at the insight you gain, the habits you learn, the imagination you develop and the community you form. One final point can help you get started on the right foot: dwelling in the Word is about hearing from God's Word and hearing from each other. Each person is responsible for helping one other person give voice to what she or he heard from the text and to then be an advocate for that person's thoughts in the larger group. These practices are intended to help the group create an environment where thoughts are safely shared and members listen deeply to one another. Over time, dwelling in the Word is a powerful tool that can form a community of the Spirit where the presence and power of the Spirit is both welcome and expected.

Practice 2: Contextual Analysis

Missionaries know that the gospel must be translated—literally and figuratively—into local contexts. Every local culture is unique and will hear and receive the gospel in different ways. A good missionary learns to understand local cultures so that he or she can inculturate the gospel in a way specifically tailored to a specific people group. At times of inculturation into new contexts, the gospel has proven to be the most effective at bringing about radical transformation in individuals, communities and whole societies. The Forge Guides for Missional Conversation are designed to help Christian communities inculturate and translate the gospel into their local contexts by facilitating shared practices of contextual analysis during group gatherings.

Practices of contextual analysis will focus on three main areas: describing the local context, discerning what God is already doing in the local context and wondering together what God might want to do in the local context. A variety of ways to practice contextual analysis are provided in each session. Sometimes the group will simply have questions to answer. At other times they will be asked to complete an activity or reflect personally. It is hoped that the variety of practices provided will lead the group to a new understanding of their context and will help the group faithfully proclaim and live out the gospel in new and exciting ways that transform the members of the group and the world around them.

Practice 3: Theological Reflection

David Kelsey defines theology as the search to understand and know God truly.[3] Theology in this sense becomes wisdom in relationship to God. Much like understanding an instruction manual about building a bike leads to the ability to build that bike, searching to understand God brings about some ability to relate with God through spiritual practices, worship and faith. Those who know God can sense and participate in what God is doing in the world around them.

The section on theological reflection is designed to help your group seek to know God truly so that the group might become wise in relationship to God. It will encourage you to actively wonder about who God is and what he is up to in the world. Scripture passages and a few reflection questions will be provided for the group to study. Sometimes other sources of theological reflection—such as distinct church traditions, church history or other texts—will be provided. No matter what specific content is provided for you to reflect on, the goal will always be the same and that is for your group to ask, What can we know about who God is and what God does? How does this influence the way we relate to God and join with him in what he is doing?

Practice 4: Missionary Imagination

Each session will conclude with a time for developing a missionary imagination through conversation, personal reflection, group affirmation, prayer or a variety of other activities. The time set aside for missionary imagination is intended to help each individual in the group gain a better sense of his or her own missionary calling, and also to help the group as a whole develop a missionary imagination for its existence. I've tried particularly hard to provide a wide variety of activities in this section. The goal of these activities as well as their very nature is meant to help you and your group break the mold when it comes to calling, vision and imagination. When my own small group went through this material, we had a blast doing things like drawing pictures, sharing stories, writing limericks and making collages, as well as answering the more conventional discussion questions. Have fun with this section and do your best to encourage one another to be imaginative, innovative and experimental in missionary living.

Before We Meet Again

Midweek assignments are given at the end of each week's session. These assignments are fun little projects designed to help group members continue to think about the session throughout the week. For instance, one assignment might ask members to take pictures of three things during the week that they think represent the work of God in the world. Time for the group to review the midweek assignment is often built into the next week's session. I strongly encourage your group to complete these assignments whenever possible. My own group really enjoyed them!

Recording and Reflecting

As your group talks through these guides, my final recommendation is to take notes during the discussions, whether individually or through a general secretary. These records will help you discern patterns and commonalities that may help you see what God is doing in your lives.

INTRODUCTION

Culture:
Living in the Places of God

The Christian church has been multicultural from the dawn of its existence. Consider, for example, the day of Pentecost in Acts 2. The Spirit came upon the followers of Christ and empowered them to speak in foreign tongues. Their multilingual preaching to the multi-ethnic crowd prompted the people from "every nation under heaven" to ask what was happening, to wonder what God was up to in this miraculous event (Acts 2:5). The "God-fearing Jews" (v. 5) who heard and responded to the words of God that day included "Parthians, Medes and Elamites; residents of Mesopotamia, Judea and Cappadocia, Pontus and Asia, Phrygia and Pamphylia, Egypt and the parts of Libya near Cyrene; visitors from Rome (both Jews and converts to Judaism); Cretans and Arabs" (Acts 2:9-11). This story, found early in Acts, signals the beginning of a theme that runs throughout the book: the gospel and church of Jesus Christ can powerfully encounter every culture in every context.

Not too long after the day of Pentecost the church was scattered throughout much of the known world, taking with it the message of the gospel and the traditions of the church (Acts 8:1-8, 26-40; 13:1-4).

The dispersion of Christians throughout the world generated questions: How should Christians encounter their new surroundings? How should they respond to Gentiles (non-Jews) who embraced the gospel message (Acts 10:1–11:26)? What practices should Gentiles be required to adopt or give up (Acts 15)? A cursory reading of Acts reveals that the early church had no clear vision for how their engagement with foreign contexts should look. Crosscultural encounters were not carefully strategized, and answers to the questions that arose were not predetermined. Instead, the Spirit initiated each encounter and thus drove theological responses. The church in Acts learned repeatedly to ask the question, Who do we need to be and what type of message do we need to speak in order to faithfully live on mission in every context we encounter?

Ever since the events recorded in Acts the church has continued to ask that question and has answered it in a variety of ways. Some have maintained that the church needs to remain separate, or counter-cultural, living in a different manner than the world and avoiding the perils of worldly things. Others have held that the church should seek to identify with culture as much as possible. Some have stressed the universal nature of the gospel, while others have focused on the ability of the gospel to be modified in order for a culture to accept it. Some have sought to remain faithful to the ancient traditions of the church in every context, while others have sought to adapt their practices to the surrounding culture.

Asking questions about the church's relationship to culture and context is of extreme importance right now in the West. Societies have changed in massively disruptive ways. Every church in the West now finds itself in a new world—a new context that forces the church into a new encounter with culture. Societies in the West are no longer presumed to be fundamentally Christian, so this new encounter the church has with the world is once again a missionary encounter. This means that the church has started to once again ask the age-old question, Who do we need to be and what type of message do we need to speak in order to faithfully live on mission in every context we encounter?

This conversation guide will help your group ask that question and will provide you with discussion starters that may help you discover how God is asking you to encounter your own context. My goal is to help you make this question your own—it is not to provide easy answers or simple steps to follow. Instead, I have outlined six conversations about the various roles I believe the church ought to play as it lives on mission and encounters cultures. These six roles are *ambassador, illuminator, translator, narrator, foreigner* and *enhancer.* I pray that your conversations challenge you to faithfully encounter your context as you develop a missionary imagination for your everyday life.

LIVING AS AMBASSADORS

Preparing People to Encounter God

The role of *ambassador* is the primary role the church plays in its encounters with cultures and contexts. An ambassador is a representative of an idea or country to another—for example, the French ambassador to Portugal. Second Corinthians 5:20 refers to the church as Christ's ambassadors, through whom God makes his appeal for the world to be reconciled to him. During this session you will begin to identify the culture and context to which you have been sent as God's ambassadors. You will also reflect on God as one who sends his people into the world to proclaim reconciliation through Jesus. Finally, you will imagine together how God might be sending you, and how, as his ambassadors, you can live as missionaries in your context through your everyday life.

Dwelling in the Word

- Begin in prayer, inviting the Spirit to guide your group as you dwell in the text.

- Read aloud Luke 10:1-20.

- After the reading has been completed, allow a few moments of silence to reflect on the passage and what stands out to you.

- Break into pairs (preferably with someone you don't know well) and discuss the following questions. Use this time to practice listening to each other as well as to the text.

  - What in the text captured your imagination?

  - What question would you most like to ask a biblical scholar?

- Gather once again as a large group and share your partners' responses.

- Review these responses and discuss: What might God be up to in the passage for us today?

Contextual Analysis

Cultures are patterned ways of life that people share and pass on to new generations. The Lausanne Consultation on Gospel and Cultures describes culture as

> an integrated system of beliefs (about God or reality or ultimate meaning), of values (about what is true, good, beautiful and normative), of customs (how to behave, relate to others, talk, pray, dress, work, play, trade, farm, eat, etc.), and of institutions which express these beliefs, values and customs (government, law courts, temples or churches, family, schools, hospitals, factories, shops, unions, clubs, etc.), which binds a society together and gives it a sense of identity, dignity, security, and continuity.[4]

This definition can make it seem like cultures are homogenous, uniting all people in a certain area into one clear and consistent manner of living. In reality, cultures are pluralistic, fragmented into various subcultures that comprise the larger whole like a patchwork quilt. One cannot, for instance, simply speak of an American culture without taking into account the various contexts Americans live in. Inner-city, urban areas are very different than suburban or rural areas. Racial and ethnic differences also contribute to cultural variety, and not just between different races or ethnicities. A predominantly black cultural context in New York City is likely to be much different than a black context in Mississippi, just as a predominantly white cultural context in California is likely to be much different than a white context in Minnesota.

Think of culture, the patterns of a way of life, as both the quilt and the patchwork—that which unites a culture and that which gives it plurality and variety. At the same time, consider context to be your location on that patchwork quilt. Your context might have many cultures and subcultures, or it may have relatively few. Your *context* is the geographical place or specific people group you have been called and sent to, while *culture* describes the ways of life within that context.

1. Based on these definitions, what is the context you feel God has called you to? Is it a specific place, neighborhood or location? Is it a certain people group, class or society?

2. List as many descriptors of your context (pertaining to both people and place) as you can.

3. Using your previous answers, describe the culture(s) and subculture(s) within your context.

4. How would you describe your current relationship to your context (outsider, insider, peer, leader, foreigner, etc.)?

How would people in your context define their relationship to you?

Theological Reflection: *The God Who Sends His Laborers*

5. Second Corinthians 5:20 refers to Christians as "ambassadors for Christ." Read 2 Corinthians 5:11–6:1. Read with the following question in mind and then discuss as a group: What does it mean to be an ambassador for Christ according to this text?

6. In Luke 10, Jesus sends his followers into various local contexts and gives them detailed instructions concerning how they are to be his ambassadors. Read Luke 10:1-20. List as many observations as you possibly can about Jesus' sending of his disciples. How did Jesus send them? Where were they sent? What instructions were they

given? What were their instructions about: demeanor or attitude?

7. Jesus often spoke about the world as a field ready for harvest. The harvest would produce fruits of righteousness that would endure eternally in God's kingdom. Jesus uses the idea of the harvest a bit differently in a parable he tells in Matthew. Read Jesus' parable (Mt 13:24-30) and his explanation of it (Mt 13:36-43). How might this parable influence the way God's people act as his ambassadors to the world?

8. Based on these texts, what can we know about who God is and what God does? How does this influence the way we relate to God and join with him in what he is doing?

Missionary Imagination: *Ambassadors Who Practice Passion*

Alan Hirsch and Mike Frost refer to the six Ps of missional living:

- Presence—an incarnational lifestyle that practices the presence of Christ in the world by investing in a given culture or people group, identifying with them and taking their concerns to heart.

- Proximity—immersing oneself relationally with a people or culture, entering their lives, sharing their experiences and spending significant time with them.

- Powerlessness—giving up our sense of power and control and all the things that go with them by assuming a posture of need, living as humble missionaries to our contexts.

- Prevenience—believing God is already at work in the world and is revealing himself to people who are not yet Christian, discerning where God is working, and joining God in that work.

- Passion—suffering for the sake of Christ, bearing the cross, paying the cost of discipleship by empathizing with and entering into the pain of broken contexts.

- Proclamation—announcing the good news of the kingdom of God brought near through Jesus Christ and made available through the Holy Spirit.[5]

9. Compare this list to the instructions Jesus gave to his followers. What correlations exist between the two? How well do the six Ps identify with Jesus' instructions?

10. Assume for the time being that any ambassador for Christ would need to practice all six Ps. Which practices are you already doing well? Which would you need to develop in order to fulfill your role as ambassador?

Concerning the practice of passion, Alan and Debra Hirsch write:

The fact is that humans suffer, and Christians who take seriously the lost and broken in our world will also suffer. This is the cost of discipleship. . . . This, in our minds, squares with how Jesus responded to others. He not only identified by experiencing the limitation that humanity brought, but he extended himself to feel what the other was feeling. We have called this an *incarnation of the heart,* and believe it is essential if we are to embody what it is to be like Jesus and to offer this gift to the rest of humanity.[6]

11. What would the practice of passion look like in your context?

Before We Meet Again

- Translate Jesus' instructions to his disciples in Luke 10 into your context for your group. Write a new set of instructions that Jesus might give your group as he sends you into the world. Be prepared to share your instructions at the next group meeting.

- On two note cards, write two definitions (one on each), one for what it means to be an ambassador and another for what it means to practice passion. Flip the cards over and design two simple symbols: one that represents your group being ambassadors and another that represents your group practicing passion. Keep these cards near your Bible. Each time you read and reflect on the Scripture passages, pray that God would make the definitions on the cards to become definitions of your life. Consider the symbols you drew. Pray that God would help you envision how you can live out the symbols.

- Observe the people in your context as you go about your daily life. Try to keep three questions in mind:

    1. What type of life do the people in my context live?

    2. What clues do they give about why they live as they do?

    3. How do their lives reflect God's beauty and sin's death?

- Try to record your observations in a journal three to five times each week. Reflect on your observations after you have recorded them, and then prayerfully answer the following:

    4. What might God be up to in this person/context?

    5. How might I join God in what he is already doing?

LIVING AS
ILLUMINATORS

Shining God's Light in Every Context

God sends his people into every corner of the earth to shine his light. It does not matter how deep the darkness is in a given place, Christians are still called to shine forth God's light because, as Psalm 24:1 says, "The earth is the LORD's, and everything in it, / the world, and all who live in it." God is the Creator of everything that exists (Gen 1–2), and though sin and death have entered the world, separating people from God (Gen 3), the world remains God's and will continue to be his until every tribe, tongue and nation lives by the light of the glory of God in the New Jerusalem (Rev 21).

Since the earth has been created by God, belongs to God and will forever be God's, there is no context that is too dark or beyond reach, no culture that is inferior and no people that is too full of sin to prevent the light of God from shining. Unlike Jonah, who shunned his missionary calling out of fear that God would bring his enemies to repentance through his preaching, the church is to joyfully and willingly shine in any dark place where God sends them.

This session is designed to help you develop an imagination for how God has made you to shine his light and to help you discern where he is asking you to illumine the darkness.

Take a few moments to share your assignments and reflections since the last group meeting.

Dwelling in the Word

- Begin in prayer, inviting the Spirit to guide your group as you dwell in the text.

- Read aloud Luke 10:1-20.

- After the reading has been completed, allow a few moments of silence to reflect on the passage and what stands out to you.

- Break into pairs (preferably with someone you don't know well) and discuss the following questions. Use this time to practice listening to each other as well as to the text.

  - What in the text captured your imagination?

  - What question would you most like to ask a biblical scholar?

- Gather once again as a large group and share your partners' responses.

- Review these responses and discuss: What might God be up to in the passage for us today?

Contextual Analysis

The Bible often compares righteousness, wisdom and life with light, and wickedness, folly and death with darkness (see Ps 56:13; Prov 4:19). Assess what is light and dark in your context by answering the following questions:

1. Assume you are a missionary-minded cultural anthropologist who has just moved into your present context. What things do you think you would describe as things of light and life?

   families
   community

2. What things do you think you would describe as things of darkness and death?   *people-pleasers*

   boxed-in life
   busyness.
   competition

Theological Reflection: *The God Who Gives Light to the World*

No biblical author talked about light and darkness more than John, who repeatedly described Jesus as light and instructed the church to live in that light.

3. Break into pairs and read one of John's descriptions of Jesus as light: John 1:1-13; 8:12-20; 12:34-50. Why does John refer to Jesus as light? What is the theological significance of the reference? In other words, what does John mean by calling Jesus light?

   His being, presence showed people their
   wrongs, their sins

4. John also instructed the church to live in God's light. Read 1 John 1:5–2:11. How do we live in God's light? What connection, if any, does this have to John's description of Jesus as light?

   Showing Jesus.

5. Jesus tells his followers, "You are the light of the world. A town built on a hill cannot be hidden. Neither do people light a lamp and put it under a bowl. Instead they put it on its stand, and it gives light to everyone in the house. In the same way, let your light shine before others, that they may see your good deeds and glorify your Father in heaven" (Mt 5:14-16). Based on this passage, what do you think it means for the church to be the light of the world? How does this describe the relationship the church is to have to cultures and contexts?

We are to stand above all as a beacon for Christ

6. Break into pairs to discuss one of the following passages and report back to the whole group how one of the following texts describes the people of God as light in the world: Isaiah 58; Isaiah 60; Acts 13:44-52; 2 Corinthians 4:1-6; Ephesians 5:1-21.

7. Now that you have considered a wide variety of texts, what would you say it means for the church to be illuminators?

8. In light of the texts you have read, what can we know about who God is and what God does? How does this influence the way we relate to God and join with him in what he is doing?

Missionary Imagination: *Illuminators Who Practice Presence*

9. If you could change into light one piece of darkness around you, what would it be?

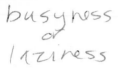

10. What might it look like for you to shed light on the dark place you would love to see changed?

In order to drive out darkness, light must shine into it—that is, the light must enter into and be in the darkness. Jesus was the light because he was present among humanity, showing us the way to God. As Jesus' followers now act as the light of the world, they must bring the presence of Christ into the world. Alan Hirsch and Debra Hirsch call this the practice of "presence," and liken it to the incarnation:

> We believe that an incarnational stance is an extremely important aspect of missional lifestyle. As God identified with us, so ought we identify with others. This will mean taking a given culture or people group seriously and deeply investing in them. We will need to take significant time to understand their history, their stories, their heroes, their books, and so on, in order to get *their* take on things. It is about immersing ourselves into their lives. When we identify with a people, we take their culture and concerns to heart.[7]

11. As a group, come up with two definitions, one for what it means to be an illuminator and another for what it means to practice

presence. Write these on two note cards (one on each). Then, come up with two symbols that are easy to draw: one that represents your group being illuminators and another that represents your group practicing presence. Draw the symbols on the opposite sides of the corresponding cards. Keep these cards near your Bible, along with the cards from session 1.

Before We Meet Again

• Continue to read and reflect on Luke 10:1-20, the passages from John and any of the texts used in this session. In the following space, record your thoughts, observations and what you hear from God.

• Look around you for examples of people who are living as light in dark places. Try to find at least two examples before your next meeting. Prepare a brief show-and-tell presentation to share what you observed with the group.

• Each time you read and reflect on the passages of this session, bring out the note cards from sessions 1-2. Pray that God would make the definitions on the cards to become definitions of your life. Next, consider the symbols you drew. Pray that God would help you envision how you can live out the symbols.

• Observe the people in your context as you go about your everyday life. Try to keep three questions in mind:

  1. What type of life do the people in my context live?

  2. What clues do they give about why they live as they do?

  3. How do their lives reflect God's beauty and sin's death?

- Try to record your observations in a journal three to five times each week. Reflect on your observations after you have recorded them and then prayerfully answer the following questions.

    4. What might God be up to in this person/context?

    5. How might I join God in what he is already doing?

- Write lyrics to the tune of "This Little Light of Mine." The lyrics should describe you or your group living as illuminators in your local context by being present with people as Jesus would be present with them. Write the lyrics in the following space. (Feel free to perform the song for your group at the start of session 3!)

Session Three

LIVING AS TRANSLATORS

Contextualizing the Gospel and the Church

The first two sessions of this book highlighted how Christians encounter cultures and contexts as ambassadors (preparing people to encounter God) and illuminators (shining God's light into *every* dark place). This third session is designed to help us think through how Christians are to live as translators by *contextualizing* the gospel and the church. *Contextualization* sounds like a fancy word, but it really only means adapting the gospel and the church so that they make sense to the local context without losing any of the fundamental, nonnegotiable elements of either gospel or church. Regarding the practice of contextualization, Angus J. L. Menuge says,

> One should not compromise the fundamental message of Christianity, but in order to communicate that message to different cultures, one can translate culture-bound ideas to their equivalents in other cultures. Christ used cultural examples drawn from agrarian Palestine to express His parables. Paul altered his

delivery and style depending on whether he was trying to reach Greeks, Romans, or Jews. C. S. Lewis claimed that his task was that of a translator, turning Christian doctrine into the vernacular of unscholarly people. Effective translation is incarnational, taking the Gospel message and finding culturally relevant clothing to express it.[8]

And Lesslie Newbigin observes,

> True contextualization happens when there is a community which lives faithfully by the gospel and in that same costly identification with people in their real situations as we see in the earthly ministry of Jesus. When these conditions are met, the sovereign Spirit of God does his own surprising work.[9]

Take a few moments to share your assignments and reflections since the last meeting.

Dwelling in the Word

- Begin in prayer, inviting the Spirit to guide your group as you dwell in the text.

- Read aloud Luke 10:1-20.

- After the reading has been completed, allow a few moments of silence to reflect on the passage and what stands out to you.

- Break into pairs (preferably with someone you don't know well) and discuss the following questions. Use this time to practice listening to each other as well as to the text.

  - What in the text captured your imagination?

  - What question would you most like to ask a biblical scholar?

- Gather once again as a large group and share your partners' responses.

- Review these responses and discuss: What might God be up to in the passage for us today?

Contextual Analysis

1. Every context encountered by the gospel and the church contains both barriers that make it difficult for people to receive the gospel or join the church, and opportunities that make it easy to capture people's interest and imagination. What barriers in your context keep people from accepting the message of Jesus' lordship or keep people from wanting to become a part of the church?

2. Where do these barriers come from? What is it about your context that raises these barriers?

3. What opportunities to capture people's interest and imagination exist within your context? In what ways are people open to the gospel and to connecting with the church?

Theological Reflection: *The God Who Makes Himself Known Throughout the Earth*

The book of Acts could be a case study for how the gospel and the church encounter new contexts and new cultures. At each new encounter the gospel was proclaimed in a nuanced way and the church reviewed and at times modified its practices. We see both the gospel and the church contextualized in the book of Acts, meaning that the earliest Christians realized that the good news of Jesus Christ and the believers who followed him might look different in every context, yet remain fundamentally united in Christ.

4. Break into pairs and read one of the following texts: Acts 13:13-43; 17:16-34; 26:1-29. In the text you chose, identify Paul's audience and what you might know about them. Share your observations with the group, then together compare and contrast Paul's presentations. How does he translate the basic message of the gospel for each context?

5. In Acts, the church quickly discovered that it had to translate not only the gospel but also itself—its rituals, practices, structures and requirements for belonging. Read Acts 10:1–11:26; 15:1-35. What changes did the church need to make as it encountered new cultures and contexts? In what ways did the church translate itself so that it might include new kinds of people?

6. Based on these texts, what can we know about who God is and what God does? How does this influence the way we relate to God and join with him in what he is doing?

Missionary Imagination: *Translators Who Practice Proclamation*

As Paul is preaching to the Athenian philosophers in Acts 17, it seems as though the crowd is with him until he begins to discuss the resurrection of the dead. When the philosophers heard Paul speak of the resurrection, "some of them sneered" (v. 32). The idea of the resurrection was a barrier that prevented the "educated elite" from responding to the gospel, but it was a nonnegotiable feature of Paul's message.

7. Together, outline the nonnegotiable elements of the gospel that you must proclaim no matter how offensive or ridiculous they might seem to your context.

8. Notice, however, that not everyone sneered at Paul's message. Some were intrigued and asked to hear more (v. 32). Paul had successfully used his observation of their cultural ways to pique their interest in Jesus and his resurrection. What opportunities does your culture or context provide for piquing people's interest in the gospel? How might you use those opportunities?

9. Imagine that you encounter a group of people who represent your culture, as the philosophers represented the culture of Athens. Prepare an outline of a contextualized proclamation of the gospel to this group of people that takes note of both the barriers and

opportunities you have previously discussed. Record the outline your group develops in the following space. Each group member will be asked to fill out the outline before the next meeting.

10. Divide into two groups and prepare two skits of 2-3 minutes. One group should produce a skit that reflects a church that has intentionally been contextualized for your local context. The other group's skit should reflect a noncontextualized church. After each group has presented its skit, discuss how well the skits represent contextualized and noncontextualized churches in your area.

11. As you conclude this session, share with each other ways you are feeling led to translate the gospel and the church for the people around you.

Before We Meet Again

- Continue to read and reflect on Luke 10:1-20, Paul's sermons or any of the texts used in this session. In the following space, record your thoughts, observations and what you hear from God.

- Scan through the book of Galatians, a letter Paul wrote to churches that had been swayed into thinking that people must become culturally Jewish to receive salvation. What does this letter add to the discussion about the relationship between the church and culture and the need to translate the gospel and the church into every culture? (Pay particular attention to Galatians 1:6–2:14; 5:1-12; 6:12-16.)

- Write two definitions, one for what it means to be a translator and another for what it means to practice proclamation. Write these definitions on two note cards. Then come up with two symbols that are easy to draw: one that represents your group being translators and another that represents your group practicing proclamation. Draw these symbols on the reverse of their respective definitions. Pray that God would make the definitions on the cards to become definitions of your life. Next, consider the symbols you drew. Pray that God would help you envision how you can live out the symbols.

- Fill in the outline your group developed of a contextualized proclamation of the gospel (see question 9). Try to write the proclamation in at least five hundred words. Be prepared to read your presentation at the next group meeting.

- Try to observe the people in your context as you go about your everyday life. Keep three questions in mind:

    1. What type of life do the people in my context live?

    2. What clues do they give about why they live as they do?

    3. How do their lives reflect God's beauty and sin's death?

- Try to record your observations in a journal three to five times each week. Reflect on your observations after you have recorded them, and then prayerfully answer the following:

    4. What might God be up to in this person/context?

    5. How might I join God in what he is already doing?

LIVING AS NARRATORS

Changing the Social Story

Storytelling may not seem like a missional practice, but it is in fact crucial to faithfully living out our missionary calling. Storytelling is essential because narratives matter so much to cultures and contexts. Indeed, it would be impossible for people to share common ways of life if they did not also share some sort of common narrative, some kind of social story to shape the way they view life, themselves, their relationships to one another and to the world.

Christians live by a story that differs decidedly from the stories of the world. The Christian's story is epic, a celebration of the Creator God whose mighty deeds have accomplished salvation for his people, culminating in God's eternal reign over his kingdom. It is a story built on faith, a story that sustains hope and a story expressed in love. It is a story that offers Christians a common understanding that leads to common practices. It is a story that encounters all other stories and challenges them to be retold in light of God's actions in history.

Living as missionaries sent to encounter other cultures and contexts requires acting as narrators who tell a different story about history,
life, the future and the world. You will, during this session, begin to
think about the stories that shape the lives of the people around you,
the story that shapes you, and how you can faithfully narrate God's
story in a way that invites all who hear it to make it their own.

Break into pairs and share the gospel proclamation you prepared after
session 3.

Dwelling in the Word

- Begin in prayer, inviting the Spirit to guide your group as you dwell
  in the text.

- Read aloud Luke 10:1-20.

- After the reading has been completed, allow a few moments of silence to reflect on the passage and what stands out to you.

- Break into pairs (preferably with someone you don't know well)
  and discuss the following questions. Use this time to practice listening to each other as well as to the text.

  - What in the text captured your imagination?

  - What question would you most like to ask a biblical scholar?

- Gather once again as a large group and share your partners' responses.

- Review these responses and discuss: What might God be up to in
  the passage for us today?

Contextual Analysis

The philosopher Charles Taylor believes that the social imaginary
plays a profound role in the way people live together. He defines the
social imaginary as "the ways in which [people] imagine their social
existence . . . the way ordinary people 'imagine' their social sur-

roundings . . . that common understanding which makes possible common practices."[10] The social imaginary is both a *product* derived from the beliefs, stories, artifacts and so forth of the culture and a *producer* of the understanding people use to guide their participation in social life. The social imaginary is both the story and the author of a culture.

1. How would you describe the social story (or social imaginary) that people in your context live by?

2. What sources (relationships, institutions, media, artifacts, etc.) are most responsible for shaping and communicating this social story?

3. How is the social story/imaginary lived out? What common practices stem from the common understanding?

Theological Reflection: *The God Who Shapes Our Story*

The resurrected Jesus' encounters with two disillusioned disciples on the road to Emmaus and with the larger group of disciples provide excellent examples of how the church can live on mission in every culture and context. Read the story of Jesus' encounters:

4. Break into pairs. Read Luke 24:13-35. Make a list of each thing
   Jesus does, no matter how small the action might seem. How do
   these things help to reshape the story his disciples were living by?
   How does he change their view of history?

5. How might Jesus' actions in these passages inform the church
   how to conduct itself in various cultures and contexts?

6. Split into three groups. Compare Jesus' walk on Emmaus to his
   interaction with Nicodemus in John 3:1-21, his conversation with
   the Samaritan woman in John 4:4-26, and a portion of his Sermon
   on the Mount found in Matthew 5:13-48. How does Jesus go about
   changing the story people live by? Based on Jesus' practices, how
   might these stories add to or modify your model of mission?

Missiologists in recent years have used texts like Jesus' walk to
Emmaus to suggest various descriptions of the mission of the church.
Some call mission a journey of accompaniment, walking with people
as they journey toward Jesus. Others emphasize mutuality, solidarity,
marginality and hospitality. Most recently the focus has been on dialogue. Mission is being described as dialogue with the poor, with cultures, with religions and with our neighbors. Dialogue is practicing

conversation, a give and take that requires listening and speaking, learning and proclamation.

> Missional engagement is not homogenous; there is no one-size-fits-all pattern. Instead we must enter the local community and sit with the people, to enter and be shaped by their narratives in order to ask the question of what God may be up to in that context. . . . [T]he task of the local church in our present situation is to reenter our neighborhoods, to dwell with and to listen to the narratives and stories of the people. *We are to do this not as a strategy for getting people to church but because that is how God comes to us in Jesus.*[11]

7. In what ways do the actions of accompaniment, solidarity, mutuality and dialogue reflect who God is and how God comes to us in Jesus?

8. Based on today's conversation and readings, what can we know about who God is and what God does? How does this influence the way we relate to God and join with him in what he is doing?

Missionary Imagination: *Narrators Who Practice Proximity*

Consider the following quote from Graham Ward about the role theology plays in cultural transformation:

> In a sense what theology then aspires to facilitate . . . is an interpretation by Christ of culture's own dreaming. Theology's task

with respect to culture is to allow for that searching by Christ, in Christ, of the cultural imaginary. This is a reading of the signs of the times not just for the Church . . . but for the times themselves, so that culture itself might begin to understand its own aspirations and limitations, the hope for which it longs and the depths of fallenness into which it continually commits itself.[12]

9. How would the gospel interpret the predominant dreams in your context? How can you help your context dream differently? Live a different story?

The actions of Jesus on the road to Emmaus have become a model for mission because they exemplify the practice of proximity. Jesus walked with his followers, listened to their perspectives, spoke truth into their story, stayed with them and ate with them. Jesus changed their story, as he had previously done for many others, by proximity—being close—even if just for a few brief moments. Michael Frost believes Christians are to emulate this practice.

So, if we take the Incarnation seriously, we must take seriously the call to live incarnationally—right up close, near to those whom God desires to redeem. We cannot demonstrate Christlikeness at a distance from those who we feel called to serve. We need to get close enough to people that our lives rub up against their lives, and that they see the incarnated Christ in our values, beliefs, and practices as expressed in cultural forms that make sense and convey impact.[13]

10. How can you practice proximity with the people in your context? How can you ensure your life rubs up against theirs in such a way that you can narrate a new story to them?

11. As a group, write two definitions, one for what it means to be a narrator and another for what it means to practice proximity. Write each on a different note card. Then, come up with two symbols that are easy to draw: one that represents your group being narrators and another that represents your group practicing proximity. Draw the symbols on the reverse side of their corresponding cards. Keep these cards with those from sessions 1-3.

Before We Meet Again

- Continue to read and reflect on Luke 10:1-20 or any of the texts used in this session. In the following space, record your thoughts, observations and what you hear from God.

- Practice proximity with at least one person in your context. Make time in your schedule and be creative in finding a way to enter the person's life. Record your efforts and be prepared to discuss your experience at the next group meeting.

- Keep near your Bible the two note cards you made during this session, along with the note cards from previous sessions. Each time you read and reflect on this session's Scripture passages, pray that God would make the definitions on the cards to become defi-

nitions of your life. Next, consider the symbols you drew. Pray that
God would help you envision how you can live out the symbols.

- Try to observe the people in your context as you go about your
everyday life. Keep three questions in mind:

    1. What type of life do the people in my context live?

    2. What clues do they give about why they live as they do?

    3. How do their lives reflect God's beauty and sin's death?

- Try to record your observations in a journal three to five times each
week. Reflect on your observations after you have recorded them,
and then prayerfully answer the following:

    4. What might God be up to in this person/context?

    5. How might I join God in what he is already doing?

Session Five

LIVING AS FOREIGNERS

Belonging to a Different Realm

Scripture clearly teaches that in its missionary encounters the church is never to fully identify with the broader culture. The church is not to feel at home in this world or to strive to be a culturally elite establishment. Instead, the church is to understand that it belongs to God and his kingdom, and is therefore not of this world. This understanding means that the life of the church is one of pilgrimage and journey, of being exiles and strangers, of being foreigners in a land that is not their own.

This session is designed to help you discover what it looks like to live as a foreigner and to practice the powerlessness that comes with being foreigners. Don't forget that the ultimate goal of each session is to help us develop an imagination for how we might live as missionaries. Keep that in mind as we consider the calling of the church to live out its mission by being foreigners in the world.

Take time to share your assignments and reflections since session 4.

Dwelling in the Word

- Begin in prayer, inviting the Spirit to guide your group as you dwell in the text.

- Read aloud Luke 10:1-20.

- After the reading has been completed, allow a few moments of silence to reflect on the passage and what stands out to you.

- Break into pairs (preferably with someone you don't know well) and discuss the following questions. Use this time to practice listening to each other as well as to the text.

  - What in the text captured your imagination?

  - What question would you most like to ask a biblical scholar?

- Gather once again as a large group and share your partners' responses.

- Review these responses and discuss: What might God be up to in the passage for us today?

Contextual Analysis

Christians, according to the Bible, do not belong to the world but to God, who has selected us, called us and sent us into the world to participate in his mission. Christians are not citizens of this world, but are pilgrims on a journey toward our home in God's eternal kingdom. The allegiance of the Christian is always first to God and to his reign.

1. Complete the following comparison: Christians belong to God, as people in my context belong to _____. Explain your response.

America
Place / Placement
Desire
Grief | Doubt | Addiction | Anxiety

The jump is/and too terribly difficult

2. What is the end of the journey for people in your context? On what have they fixed their hopes and dreams?

Healing   Feeling   A New, Better World
Justice   Answers   Cure
(list could go on and on)

3. What might change about your context if people more fully realized a sense of belonging to God and his eternal kingdom?

Intrinsically, the they listed above...
A transcendent way of thinking (not A or B ... C)

Theological Reflection: *The God to Whom We Belong*

Jesus teaches his disciples repeatedly in the book of John that they belong to God and not the world. The disciples learn that God has selected and called them, and through Jesus they know God. The world, on the other hand, has not known God because it refuses to know Jesus. Therefore, the disciples are warned to not belong to the world, and to know that the world will very likely treat them as it treated Jesus.

4. Break into pairs. First, read Jesus' teaching to the disciples in John 15:18–16:4. Then read his prayer for the disciples in John 17:1-26. How does Jesus ask his followers to live? Why does he want them to live this way? What will be the outcomes of their lives if they follow his teachings?

5. Now read the teachings of how Christians are to relate to the world
   in 1 John 2:15-17 and 1 John 4:3-21. What did you learn about
   living in the world and living in God? What has this to do with the
   way the missional church encounters cultures and contexts?

   ✱ I do thin by put down "counter-cultural" a little too much. However, this, b.c. counter-cultural often gets militant!

Despite the fact that the church very clearly does not belong to the
world and is not to follow the ways or teachings of the world, Jesus
did not pray that God would take his followers out of the world but
that the world would know God and become one with God through
the way his followers lived within it. The church has always had to
live in the tension of belonging to God but living in the world. Even
naming the tension has been a struggle. Some say the church is to be
countercultural, some say acultural, and yet others liken the church
to a subcultural ghetto (think Chinatown). The best description I
have found is the church as a "parallel culture." Mary Jo Leddy compares the nature of the church to a parallel culture by drawing from
the example of the movement led by Václav Havel that eventually led
to a revolution in the Czech Republic.

Havel and the other dissidents believed that the communist system
they lived in was built on a lie, but it was a lie that they lived in and
therefore it lived in them—until they asked an important question.
"How can we live the truth in a culture based on a fundamental lie,
especially since the lie is in our heads? How can we begin to live into
the truth?" Havel's answer was to form a "parallel culture." Leddy
writes, "It was not a counter-culture because, he said, it was impossible for us to live totally outside the system. You cannot live outside
a culture. But you can create within it zones and spaces, where you
can become who you really are." For Havel, pursuing the truth
through reading groups, philosophy, poetry and art gradually, over a
period of years, wore away the power of the lie he and other dissi-

[handwritten: Not sure if "parallel" is perfect. "Yeast"?]

dents lived in, until one day, no one believed the lie anymore.[14]

6. In what ways do you think a "parallel culture" is a good description of the church's relationship to culture? How does it help you define what you feel the relationship ought to be?

[handwritten: Apart yet a insider]

[handwritten: Different but not entirely Shows the beauty & necessity of adaptation (City on hill / Salt)]

7. Based on today's conversations, what can we know about who God is and what God does? How does this influence the way we relate to God and join with him in what he is doing?

[handwritten: Jesus (back to Incarnational)]

Missionary Imagination: *Foreigners Who Practice Powerlessness*

Cathy Ross describes the experience of contextual missionaries as

> mutuality among those with whom they live; solidarity as they begin to understand and empathize with the issues in that context; marginality as they are inevitably on the margins of a new culture; transformation as they become vulnerable in new environments; being a stranger with needs as they enter the new context as outsiders and finally the joy of hospitality offered and received.[15]

There are six elements present in Ross's analysis: mutuality, solidarity, marginality, transformation, being a stranger and hospitality. Break into pairs and assign each group one or two elements, depending on your group size. Each group should answer the following:

8. What is a good example of how your assigned element has been put into practice by someone in the past?

9. How can you model your assigned element (mutuality, solidarity, marginality, transformation, being a stranger or hospitality) as a form of powerlessness?

As a missionary to your local context you are to be a foreigner that practices powerlessness. Hirsch and Hirsch say the missionary practice of powerlessness

> means that we come very humbly among a group of people. Like Jesus, we don't come into town wielding a sword . . . or riding in like the cavalry. Nor do we come legislating people's morals or flouting celebrity, money, and ego. Rather, we come to subvert evil and brokenness through Christlike service. Following our humble lord, we can never approach incarnational mission from an arrogant perspective. Missional disciples must not expect to conquer by power or force; they must use the same means as Jesus: steadfastness in truth, acceptance of being misunderstood and rejected, and a willingness to achieve victory through redemptive suffering.[16]

10. As a group, come up with two definitions, one for what it means to be a foreigner and another for what it means to practice powerlessness. Write these on note cards as before. Next, come up with two symbols that are easy to draw: one that represents your group

being foreigners and another that represents your group practicing powerlessness. Draw these on the reverse side of your cards. Keep these cards with your cards from sessions 1-4.

Before We Meet Again

- Continue to read and reflect on Luke 10:1-20, Jesus' prayer in John 17 or any of the texts used in this session. In the following space, record your thoughts, observations and what you hear from God.

- Consider the following verses: Romans 12:2; Colossians 2:8; 2:20–3:10; James 1:27; 4:4-10; 2 Peter 1:3-9. Summarize the way these texts say the Christian ought to relate to the world.

- Write a limerick that describes what it looks like to live as a foreigner and practice powerlessness in your context. If you are not familiar with this style of poetry, research the form online. Be prepared to share your limerick at your next group meeting.

- Keep the two note cards you made during this session near your Bible, along with the note cards from previous sessions. Each time you read and reflect on this session's passages, pray that God would make the definitions you wrote on your cards definitions of your life. Next, consider the symbols you drew. Pray that God would help you envision how you can live out the symbols.

- Try to observe the people in your context as you go about your everyday life. Keep three questions in mind:

  1. What type of life do the people in my context live?

  2. What clues do they give about why they live as they do?

  3. How do their lives reflect God's beauty and sin's death?

- Try to record your observations in a journal three to five times each week. Reflect on your observations after you have recorded them, and then prayerfully answer the following:

  4. What might God be up to in this person/context?

  5. How might I join God in what he is already doing?

LIVING AS ENHANCERS

Bringing Out the Beautiful

Jesus declared to his followers that they were the "salt of the earth." As the salt of the earth the church enhances the world around it, bringing more vibrancy to that which is beautiful and preserving that which is good. It also keeps the ugly and the evil at bay. The role of the enhancer is simple: make the good even better and minimalize the bad.

We must learn to see the beauty in a wide variety of cultures and contexts if we are to fill the role of enhancer. Enhancing cultures and contexts requires a view of the world that recognizes beauty in diversity and refuses to believe in the superiority of one cultural system over another. Enhancers do not seek to replace one culture with another or to transform one culture into another, but to help cultures and contexts reflect the beauty of God in every way possible. God has given culture as a gift to his people so they might peacefully and meaningfully live together. Enhancers help to ensure that each culture and context might also be a gift pleasing to God.

Share your limericks and reflections from session 5.

Dwelling in the Word

- Begin in prayer, inviting the Spirit to guide your group as you dwell in the text.
- Read aloud Luke 10:1-20.
- Allow a few moments of silence after the reading has been completed to reflect on the passage and what stands out to you.
- Break into pairs (preferably with someone you don't know well) and discuss the following questions. Use this time to practice listening to each other as well as to the text.
  - What in the text captured your imagination?
  - What question would you most like to ask a biblical scholar?
- Gather once again as a large group and share your partners' responses.
- Review these responses and discuss: What might God be up to in the passage for us today?

Contextual Analysis

"Because men and women are God's creatures, some of their culture is rich in beauty and goodness. Because they are fallen, all of it is tainted with sin and some of it is demonic."[17]

Imagine that a revival broke out in your context and massive numbers of people received the gospel and began faithfully living as followers of Christ. People's lives change to such an extent that the entire local context begins to shift in noticeable ways.

1. What beautiful and good things about your context would become even better?

2. What tainted things would be transformed and redeemed for God's glory? *turn it around —*

Ause it for your glory.

3. What demonic and evil things would be destroyed?

bondage of sin, of the past.

Theological Reflection: *The God Who Makes All Things New*

Salt, in Jesus' time, had at least four uses based on its natural qualities: preserving, purifying, seasoning and fertilizing.

4. Discuss each of the four uses of salt as it might relate to the way the church ought to encounter cultures and contexts. How does the church act as a preserver, purifier, seasoning or fertilizer in cultures and contexts?

The Lausanne Committee for World Evangelization (LCWE) commissioned a study on the relationship between the church and culture in the 1970s. The outcome of that commission was "The Willowbank Report: Consultation on Gospel and Culture." The report included the following about engaging with cultures and contexts:

> We are to challenge what is evil and affirm what is good . . . in art, science, technology, agriculture, industry, education, community development and social welfare. . . . Of course, the church cannot impose Christian standards on an un-

willing society, but it can commend them by both argument and example.[18]

The report then refers to paragraph 10, "Evangelism and Culture," of the Lausanne Covenant, which states:

> Culture must always be tested and judged by Scripture. Because men and women are God's creatures, some of their culture is rich in beauty and goodness. Because they are fallen, all of it is tainted with sin and some of it is demonic. The gospel does not presuppose the superiority of any culture to another, but evaluates all cultures according to its own criteria of truth and righteousness, and insists on moral absolutes in every culture. Missions have all too frequently exported with the gospel an alien culture and churches have sometimes been in bondage to culture rather than to Scripture. Christ's evangelists must humbly seek to empty themselves of all but their personal authenticity in order to become the servants of others, and churches must seek to transform and enrich culture, all for the glory of God. (Mark 7:8, 9, 13; Gen. 4:21, 22; 1 Cor. 9:19-23; Phil. 2:5-7; 2 Cor. 4:5)[19]

5. Respond to the two statements from the LCWE. What do you think the statements get right? What do they possibly miss or get wrong? How well do the statements help to define the church as the salt of the earth that acts as an enhancer of cultures and contexts?

Christians and churches in the New Testament are frequently admonished to stand firm (see, for example, 1 Cor 16:13; Gal 5:1; Phil

1:27; 4:1; 1 Thess 3:8; 2 Thess 2:15). Perhaps the most well-known occasion where the Christian is told to stand firm is Ephesians 6:10-18.

6. Read Ephesians 6:10-18. Considering this text, what do you think standing firm has to do with encountering cultures? How does standing firm modify your understanding of the church as an enhancer of cultures and contexts?

7. Based on these texts, what can we know about who God is and what God does? How does this influence the way we relate to God and join with him in what he is doing?

Missionary Imagination: *Enhancers Who Practice Prevenience*

Read Lesslie Newbigin's perspective on the church as enhancers of cultures:

> We are called neither to a simple affirmation of human culture nor to a simple rejection of it. We are to cherish human culture as an area in which we live under God's grace and are given daily new tokens of that grace. But we are called also to remember that we are part of that whole seamless texture of human culture which was shown on the day we call Good Friday to be in murderous rebellion against the grace of God. We have to say both "God accepts human culture" and also "God judges human culture." There will have to be room in the Christian life for the two attitudes which Von Hügel used to call the homely and the

heroic. Christian discipleship can never be all homeliness nor all heroism. It has to have elements of both and it has to learn from day to day when to accept the homely duties of life as it is, and when to take the heroic road of questioning and challenging the accepted ways. . . . What is needed is the discernment to know, from day to day and from issues to issues, when the one stance is appropriate and when the other.[20]

8. Discuss as a group how you feel you are called to be "homely" and "heroic" in your context.

9. In what ways do you feel called to challenge accepted norms and structures in your context? In what ways do you feel called to accept cultural norms and structures?

10. Together as a group, draw a large before-and-after picture of your context on poster board. The picture should depict your context as it now is and what it might look like when enhanced by the gospel. Be sure to include in the picture your group working as enhancers.

As a missionary to your local context you are to be an enhancer that practices prevenience. Practicing prevenience essentially means believing God is at work in the local context, discerning how he is at work, and joining him in that to help people encounter God. Alan Hirsch and Debra Hirsch make this practice fundamentally a belief about God:

> The truth is that God doesn't limit his presence to baptized Christians—he is an unrelenting evangelist. He is always at work in his world—right in the thick of things—in sinful people's lives, including our own. . . . John Wesley called this reality "prevenient grace" (preparatory grace). . . . He really believed that God was always preparing the way for the preaching of the gospel, that he was *at work in every person, wooing them into relationship in and through Jesus.*[21]

Prevenient = comes before coming

11. Discuss where you believe God is at work in your context and in the lives of people in your context. How do you think God is asking you to join him in his work?

12. As a group, come up with two definitions, one for what it means to be an enhancer and another for what it means to practice prevenience. Write your definitions on note cards. Then come up with two symbols that are easy to draw: one that represents your group being enhancers and another that represents your group practicing prevenience. Draw the symbols on the reverse of their corresponding cards. Keep these cards with your others from sessions 1-5.

Final Assignments

- Continue to read and reflect on Luke 10:1-20 or any text used in this session. Record your thoughts, observations and what you hear from God here:

Read Revelation 1–3 as if the letters to the seven churches were case studies in how the church is to encounter the world. What is praised? What is condemned? What do these praises and condemnations teach about how God desires his people to live?

- Keep the two note cards you made during this session near your Bible, along with the note cards from previous sessions. Each time you read and reflect on this session's Scripture passages, pray that God would make the definitions on the cards to become definitions of your life. Next, consider the symbols you drew. Pray that God would help you envision how you can live out the symbols.

- Try to observe the people in your context as you go about your everyday life. Keep three questions in mind:

  1. What type of life do the people in my context live?

  2. What clues do they give about why they live as they do?

  3. How do their lives reflect God's beauty and sin's death?

- Try to record your observations in a journal three to five times each week. Reflect on your observations after you have recorded them, and then prayerfully answer the following:

  4. What might God be up to in this person/context?

5. How might I join God in what he is already doing?

- Schedule a finale for your group. Share a meal at the event and have some fun making some kind of craft (poster, T-shirt, bookmark, birdhouse, flag) that incorporates all the symbols you drew during your use of this conversation guide. Use the craft as a reminder of how you are to encounter cultures and contexts. (Note that this kind of project is a great way to incorporate gifts and talents that don't typically get to be used during a Bible study. Who in your group would be the best person to plan it?)

- It is often said that teaching is the best form of learning. Therefore, identify 2-6 other people in your life who you could take through the material covered during your study or the key learning you gleaned from the conversations. Use this conversation guide or create your own process to take your friends through a learning journey with you.

TIPS FOR HAVING GREAT
SMALL GROUP GATHERINGS

The following tips were gleaned from my experience in small group ministry. Practice these over the course of your time together, but know they are not exhaustive. Space has been left at the end for your group to add its own tips for having great small group gatherings.

TIP 1: *Be Prepared*

Group gatherings flourish when folks come prepared. If there is one person designated to lead or facilitate the gathering, that person should be in prayer throughout the week, asking God's Spirit to lead him or her and to be present at the gathering. The leader or facilitator should also personally work through the material a couple of times so he or she can create a gathering that flows smoothly and achieves the desired objectives.

It is also important for group members to come prepared. Their preparation includes completing midweek assignments, bringing required materials, opening their minds to what God might want to say and opening their lives to where the Spirit might want to lead.

TIP 2: *Foster Habits That Create Good Conversation and Discussion*

There is a reason these guides have been titled Forge Guides for Missional Conversation. They are meant to *create conversation* about living missionally! It is important that groups foster habits that help create good conversation. These habits include:

- Directing discussion toward all group members, not just the facilitator. Often when someone responds to a question, he or she will look at the person who asked the question. Group members should look at and interact with one another while giving their responses, not just the leader.

- Avoid the silent head nod, which is one of the biggest conversation killers. Unfortunately, it is a hard habit to break. However, when someone shares or offers a response, the group should work to give more of a response than the silent nod. Perhaps someone could ask a question, share their own insight, request for the person to say more or even just say thanks.

- Ask good questions and follow-up questions. The questions provided for you in the conversation guides will hopefully be effective at sparking conversations. It is imperative that the group does not merely answer the questions provided but asks new questions as the conversation continues. Asking new questions is a good indication that group members are listening to one another and taking an active interest in what is being said.

- Draw answers out of each participant. One of the cardinal sins of teaching or leading a discussion is to answer your own question to avoid the awkward silence. If a question is asked and no one answers after you have allowed for a comfortable time of silence, consider repeating or rephrasing the question. Also consider calling on a specific person to answer. Most of the time the person called on will have something insightful to share. I often am amazed at what the quietest people in groups have to say when a leader calls on them to specifically share. As a last resort, suggest that the group come back to the question later, or give time for individuals to share with their neighbor before sharing with everyone.

- As much as possible, affirm what others say. People feel affirmed when their thoughts are repeated or referred to later in the discussion. When people feel affirmed, they are more likely to continue to participate in the conversation.

- Clarify or summarize what has been said. Sometimes a group member will offer a long answer or get sidetracked onto a different discussion. It is often helpful for the group leader or another member to summarize what has been said, even asking for clarity if necessary. This clarifying practice will help keep the conversation moving in a focused direction.

TIP 3: *Share Leadership and Always Give People Something to Contribute*

Small groups flourish when all members are given a chance to lead on a regular basis and when all members are expected to contribute to each gathering. Rotate leadership and facilitating responsibilities while working through this guide if at all possible. Always try to find ways to ensure everyone is bringing something to contribute, whether an activity to plan or simply a snack to share.

TIP 4: *Encourage and Affirm One Another as Much as Possible*

A little bit of affirmation goes such a long way in small groups. Telling someone he or she had a good idea, did a good job leading, brought good energy to the group or made a nice snack will encourage the

person to continue to participate in group gatherings in important
ways. Groups that are able to identify each other's strengths and to
encourage those strengths to be used more will be full of life, energy
and possibility.

TIP 5: *Create Space for Feedback*

Group gatherings will be better over the long run if the group can
create a regular rhythm of giving and receiving feedback about group
gatherings. Allowing all members to give input or offer ideas for
future gatherings will increase ownership and help craft an experience unique to the group.

RECOMMENDED RESOURCES FOR FURTHER STUDY

I've had the privilege to teach on all things related to the missional church in a wide variety of settings. It is a common occurrence for me to discover that those who joined me in the learning experience often are only aware of one small portion of the missional church movement. Most folks I meet seem to only have one or two authors or teachers who have encouraged them to think and live more missionally. Consequently, these folks often have only one or two ideas of what it might look like for a Christian or a church to think and live missionally. I always love watching their expressions of surprise and joy when I tell them that the missional church conversation has been going on for over a century and has produced hundreds of books and dozens of different ideas for what the missional church might actually look like in reality. More than anything, though, I love to watch their imaginations grow as they encounter fresh voices and new ideas.

If you would like to broaden your missional imagination even further than you have already done through this study guide, the following resources will help you.

1. "A Brief History of the Missional Church Movement." This short essay describes the growth of the missional church movement from the World Missionary Conference in Edinburgh (1910) through today, identifying a variety of sources that have funded the movement. You can find this essay online at www.ivpress.com.

2. "Helpful Resources for Developing Missional Imagination." This list of resources is given to everyone who plays a leadership role in the Forge Mission Training Network so that they can expand their own imaginations for mission and help others do the same. You can view the list at www.ivpress.com. For more information on the books, you can view my list at www.worldcat.org/profiles/luthercml3/lists/2934221.

Notes

[1]Alan Hirsch, "Defining Missional," *Leadership Journal*, fall 2008, www.christianity today.com/le/2008/fall/17.20.html.

[2]"Dwelling in the Word" is a practice developed and taught to me by Dr. Patrick Keifert of Church Innovations (www.churchinnovations.org). The instructions provided are a slightly modified version of the guide provided in Patrick Keifert and Pat Taylor Ellison, *Dwelling in the Word: A Pocket Handbook* (Minneapolis: Church Innovations Institute, 2011). For more on Dwelling in the Word, visit www.churchinnovations.org/06_about/ dwelling.html.

[3]David H. Kelsey, *To Understand God Truly: What's Theological About a Theological School?* (Louisville: Westminster/John Knox Press, 1992).

[4]"Lop2: The Willowbank Report: Consultation on Gospel and Culture," *Lausanne Occasional Papers (LOPs)*, 1978, www.lausanne.org/en/documents/lops/73-lop-2.html.

[5]For a full discussion of the six Ps, see Alan Hirsch and Debra Hirsch, *Untamed: Reactivating a Missional Form of Discipleship*, Shapevine Missional Series (Grand Rapids: Baker, 2010). See also Michael Frost, *Exiles: Living Missionally in a Post-Christian Culture* (Peabody, MA: Hendrickson, 2006).

[6]Hirsch and Hirsch, *Untamed*, p. 246.

[7]Alan Hirsch and Debra Hirsch, *Untamed: Reactivating a Missional Form of Discipleship*, Shapevine Missional Series (Grand Rapids: Baker, 2010), p. 236.

[8]Angus J. L. Menuge, "Niebuhr's *Christ and Culture* Reexamined," in *Christ and Culture in Dialogue*, eds. Angus J. L. Menuge, William R. Se Cario, Alberto R. Garcia and Dale E. Griffin (St. Louis: Concordia Publishing, 1999), www.mtio.com/articles/bissar26.htm.

[9]Lesslie Newbigin, *The Gospel in a Pluralist Society* (Grand Rapids: Eerdmans, 1989).

[10]Charles Taylor, *Modern Social Imaginaries* (Durham, NC: Duke University Press, 2004), p. 16, quoted in Graham Ward, *Cultural Transformation and Religious Practice* (New York: Cambridge University Press, 2005), p. 128.

[11]Alan J. Roxburgh and M. Scott Boren, *Introducing the Missional Church: What It Is, Why It Matters, How to Become One* (Grand Rapids: Baker, 2009), p. 85, emphasis added.

[12]Ward, *Cultural Transformation*, p. 59.

[13]Michael Frost, *Exiles: Living Missionally in a Post-Christian Culture* (Peabody, MA: Hendrickson, 2006), p. 44.

[14]Mary Jo Leddy, "The People of God as a Hermeneutic of the Gospel," in *Confident Witness—Changing World*, ed. Craig Van Gelder, The Gospel and Our Culture Series (Grand Rapids: Eerdmans, 1999), pp. 310-11.

[15]Cathy Ross, "Educating for Contextual Mission," *Colloquium* 38, no. 2 (2006): 181.

[16]Alan Hirsch and Debra Hirsch, *Untamed: Reactivating a Missional Form of Discipleship*, Shapevine Missional Series (Grand Rapids: Baker, 2010), pp. 241-42.

[17]Lausanne Covenant, para. 10, www.lausanne.org/en/documents/lausanne-covenant. html.

[18]"Lop2: The Willowbank Report: Consultation on Gospel and Culture," *Lausanne Occasional Papers (LOPs)*, 1978, www.lausanne.org/en/documents/lops/73-lop-2.html.

[19]Lausanne Covenant, para 10.

[20]Lesslie Newbigin, *The Gospel in a Pluralist Society* (Grand Rapids: Eerdmans, 1989), pp. 195-96.

[21]Alan Hirsch and Debra Hirsch, *Untamed: Reactivating a Missional Form of Discipleship*, Shapevine Missional Series (Grand Rapids: Baker, 2010), pp. 242-43.

Forge Guides
for Missional Conversation

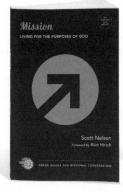

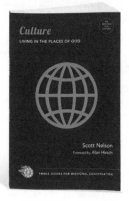

COMMUNITY: *Living as the People of God*
MISSION: *Living for the Purposes of God*
POWER: *Living by the Spirit of God*
VISION: *Living Under the Promises of God*
CULTURE: *Living in the Places of God*

Forge

How can God's people give witness to his kingdom in an increasingly post-Christian culture? How can the church recover its true mission in the face of a world in need? Forge America exists to help birth and nurture the missional church in America and beyond. Books published by InterVarsity Press that bear the Forge imprint will also serve that purpose.

Forge Books from InterVarsity Press

Creating a Missional Culture, JR Woodward

Forge Guides for Missional Conversation (set of five), Scott Nelson

The Missional Quest, Lance Ford and Brad Brisco

More Than Enchanting, Jo Saxton

The Story of God, the Story of Us, Sean Gladding

For more information on Forge America, to apply for a
Forge residency, or to find or start a Forge hub in your area,
visit **www.forgeamerica.com**

For more information about Forge books from
InterVarsity Press, including forthcoming releases,
visit **www.ivpress.com/forge**